the BIG
little book
of
work happiness

jody b. miller

TEDx Speaker, Author of "From Drift to SHIFT" and "The MISOGI Method: The Way To Achieve Lasting Happiness"

the BIG little book of work happiness

jody b. miller

TEDx Speaker, Author of "From Drift to SHIFT" and "The MISOGI Method: The Way To Achieve Lasting Happiness"

Dedication

To the love of my life.
You make work (and life) fun.

the BIG little book of work happiness

Published By
Alskar Publishing
P.O. Box 2637, Santa Barbara, CA 93120

Website: www.jodybmiller.com
Email: jody@jodybmiller.com

Layout by: JC Berry
Photos: Licensed

First published: January, 2019

ISBN-13: : 978-1-7335352-2-9
Paperback Version

the BIG little book of work happiness
written by Jody B. Miller

Also being released in 2019

the BIG little book of
relationship happiness

the BIG little book of
meditation happiness

the BIG little book of
fitness happiness

the BIG little book of
health happiness

the BIG little book of
friendship happiness

the BIG little book of
personal happiness

Alskar Publishing
U.S.A.

From the Author

The advice in this book contains decades of experience. It incorporates extensive research. You will get key pointers based on the opinions of thousands of happy and unhappy workers. And, you will gain from management perspectives from companies around the world.

If you paid a therapist to help you increase your work happiness, it would cost you a lot! Yet, much of what they tell you is in this book.

While I am not a doctor of any sort, and I must tell you that your happiness is ultimately up to you, I can attest to the power of the recommendations in this book.

I research work happiness, I write about work happiness and I speak about work happiness around the world.

And now, I am bringing you the 'best of the best' so that you can be happier at work (and in life) too.

Your work happiness is in your control.

For best results, pick and choose based on your situation and apply to your life immediately.

Repeat as needed.

Table of Contents

Cover	2
Dedication	4
Copyright	5
Also released in 2019	6
From the Author	7
Table of Contents	9
PART ONE: *Your Confidence*	11
PART TWO: *Your Work*	59
PART THREE: *Your Success*	104
About the Author	199
If you've found this book helpful…	201
the BIG little book of relationship happiness	203
Cover	205
Copyright	206
Dedication	207
Sample of Book Two	208

From the Author 209

PART ONE: Self-Love 211

PART TWO: Romance

PART THREE: Friendship

BLESSING 227

To get on the launch list for 228

the BIG little book or relationship happiness

Part One

Your Confidence

You will *never* be 100% ready.
So stop paralyzing yourself by preparing.
Just say *yes*, jump in,
and learn as you go!

Happiness is *your* responsibility.
If you practice happiness, good
things will follow you
wherever you go.

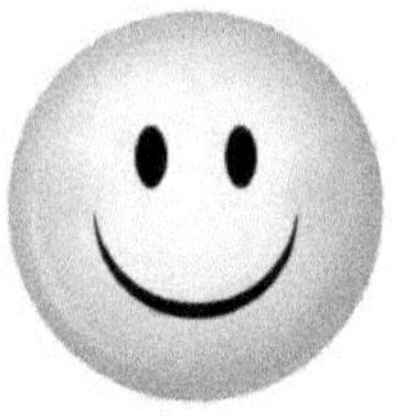

Smile more at work.
People will smile back at you and like you more.

STOP Complaining.

Thoughts become things.
Think good ones.

Let motivation drive you.

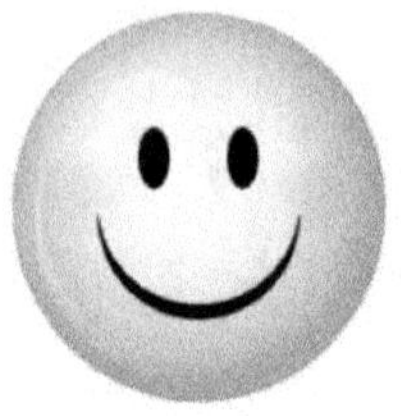

Do something you enjoy before
you go to bed.
You will sleep better and
wake up happier.

If you look for the good in yourself,
you will find it.
If you look for the good in others,
you will help them find it too.

It's always good to ask

WHY?

Why gets you closer to your purpose.

Always wear a suit to the first interview.
Always.

Listen twice as much as you talk.
You'll be amazed at what you learn.

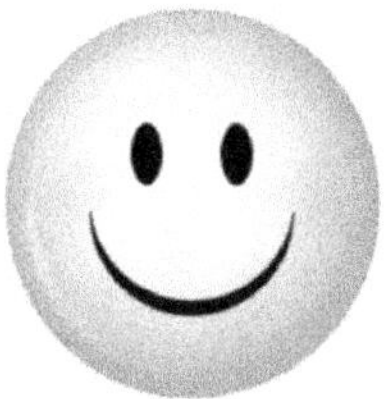

It takes less muscles to smile than it does to frown.

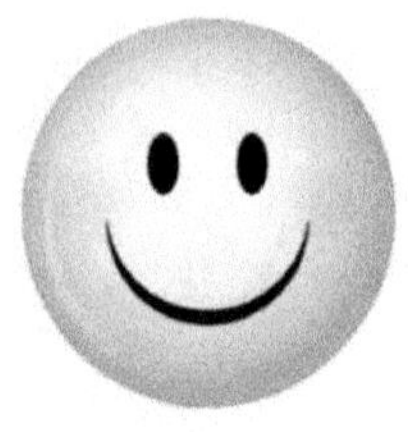

Be simple and clear in your communication. Don't fill your phrases with business speak.

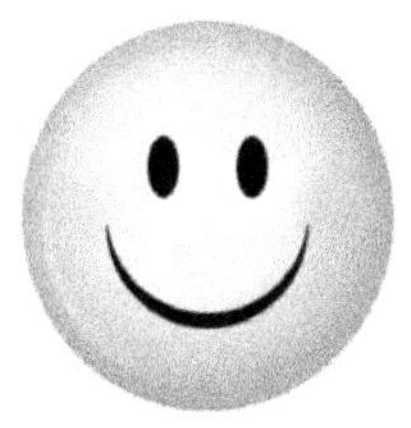

EXERCISE.

Endorphins rise and so does your happiness.

Get something on the calendar.

Your happiness will increase when
you dream about that
upcoming adventure,
event or vacation.

Your success has
nothing to do with luck.
It is all about controlled confidence.
Don't underestimate
or undermine you.

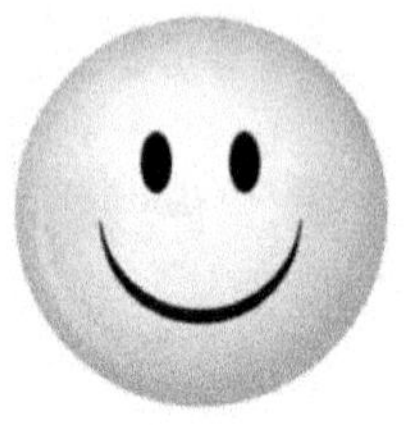

Read something different
once a week.
You will become *much* more
interesting.

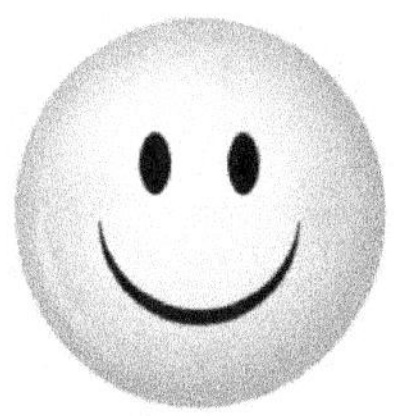

Have you figured out your *Purpose*?
Your *Passion*?
What *Motivates* you?
Once you do, you are well on your way to a very happy work life.

In the morning, practice a simple 10-minute…

MEDITATION.
Breathe in.
Breathe out.
Repeat.
Let thoughts come and let them go.
You will start your day already in flow.

Get plenty of sleep.

Don't try and imitate other people.
Be confident in you.

Worry leads to fear.
Fear leads to illness.
You don't want to get sick, do you?

If you can't stop worrying, then
worry BIG for a moment.
Think of the worst thing that could
happen with the situation
and then prepare for it.
Accept it.
Guess what?
You won't be worried anymore.
And, it probably
won't happen anyway.

If you feel tense, then get tense.
Tighten up every muscle
in your body, including
closing your eyes tightly
and making fists.

Then let it all go.
You will feel more relaxed
immediately.

Mantras make you happier.

I am a wonderful person.
I am a nice person.
Everything is always working out for me.
Good things are on their way to me.
I am a happy person.
I am a great friend.
I am a great partner.
I am a great contributor.
I like me.

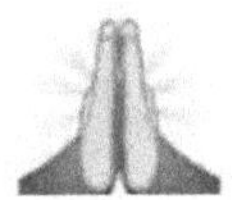

Ommmm……

If you are hungry,
your mood will suffer.
Eat something.

Start with breakfast.
Coffee isn't breakfast.

Stand up and stretch every hour.
You will feel more energized.

Shut off all the noise around you. You will improve your focus and get much more done.

Always ask for next steps when communicating.
You will drive the process forward and
will feel in control.

*"That sounds great.
What are the next steps?"*

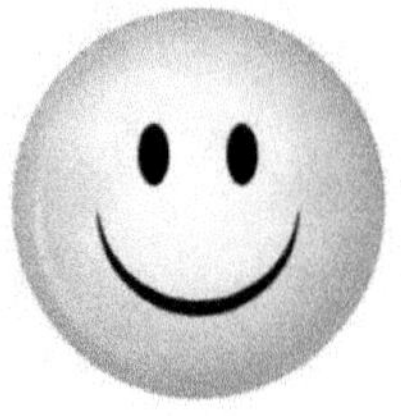

Don't focus on failure.
Focus on success.

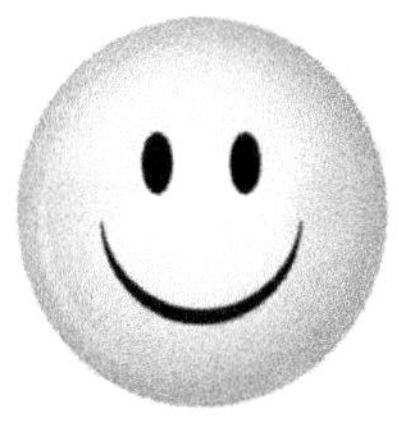

If you don't know the perfect industry or job, take a career personality test to find it.

Practice positive self-talk.
You can be your own best friend
or your own worst enemy.
Choose friend.

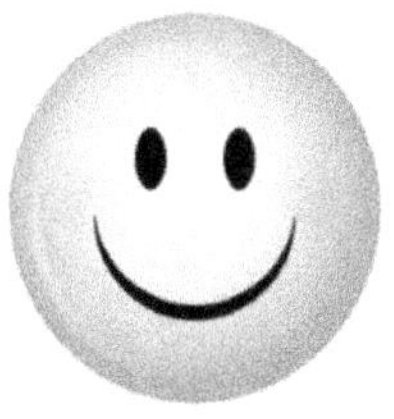

If you feel lethargic, depressed, unmotivated, bored or stressed at work.
Go for a walk.
OUTSIDE!

Nature is a natural mood booster.

Spend some time alone each day.
You will feel more balanced.

Lighten up.
Laughter is the best medicine for happiness.

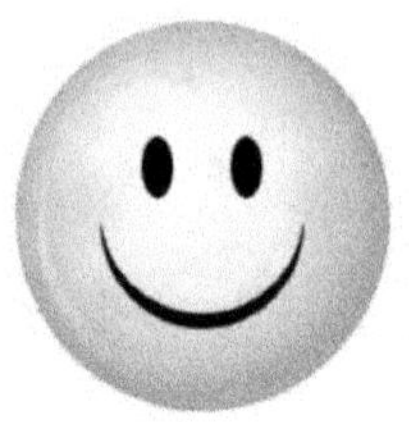

If you are a woman and others tell you to be quiet and nice, CHANGE!
More women are rising up.
It's your turn.
Take calculated risks.

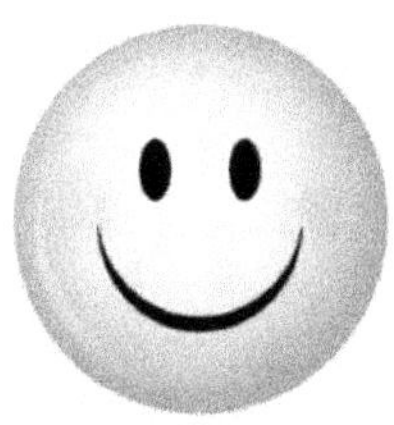

When in doubt,
take ACTION.

It takes 7 days to create a new, positive habit.
It takes 21 days for it to stick long-term.
Start a new positive habit today.

Your intuition is your guiding light.
Pay attention to it.

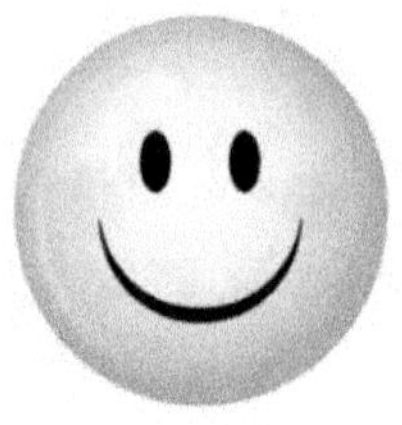

Keep a journal.
Writing helps us work out our feelings.

Step outside your comfort zone
and…
EMBRACE CHANGE.

Step to the outer limits of your comfort zone | Jody Miller | TEDxOakLawn
513,707 views

You can't control everything,
so don't try.
What a relief!

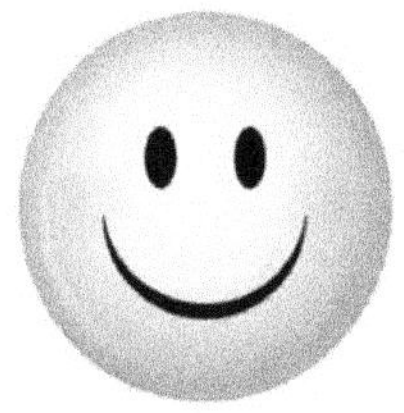

You can't please everyone.

When you please yourself,
it is not being selfish.
You will naturally be more pleasing
to others because you will emit a
happier you.

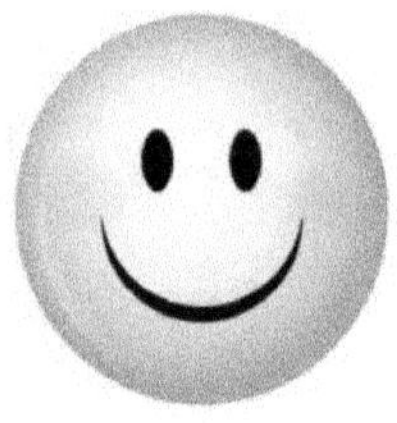

Have you ever tried yoga?
It's like going to a mind-body
happiness class.

Practice power poses.
This simple action will make you
feel more confident and
Happier right away.

If you have a positive attitude,
the world will treat you better.

Part Two

Your Work

If you treated everyone at work as
though they were the most
important person in the world –
even for one day,
you would be happier.

Why?

They will feel appreciated
and will appreciate you.

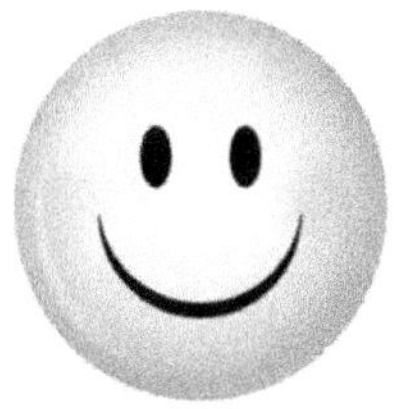

If you are unhappy at your current job, take a deep breath and talk to your boss.

Bosses are not monsters.

DisABLEd people at work are actually your best teachers. They live in the moment.

You can't change people.
So stop trying.
Instead, change yourself and
lead by example.

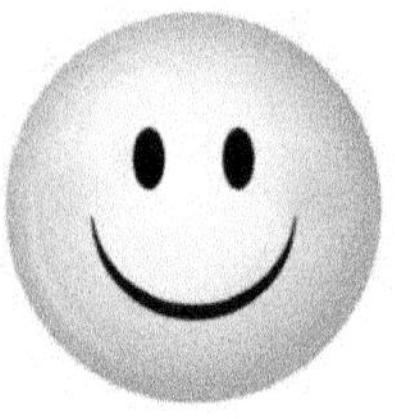

Celebrate others successes.
Curb the jealousy.

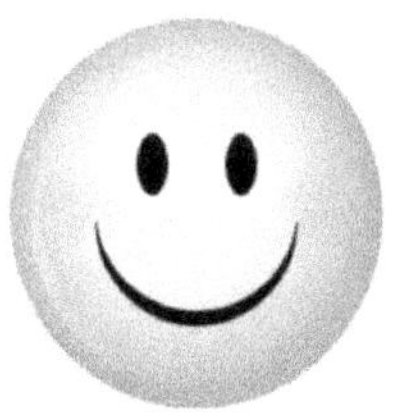

When you hate someone, you are actually giving your power to them.
Don't hate.
Don't seek revenge.
Just let it go.

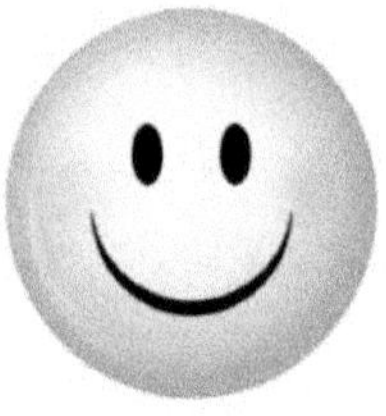

If you help others,
they will trust you *and* help you.

Want to get promoted quickly?
Remember this rule.

First in.
Last to leave.

Don't hold others responsible for
your thoughts and feelings.
You are the only one
who controls you.
Own your power.

When you are doing work that fits
your skills and goals,
you are in FLOW…
It's the best feeling!

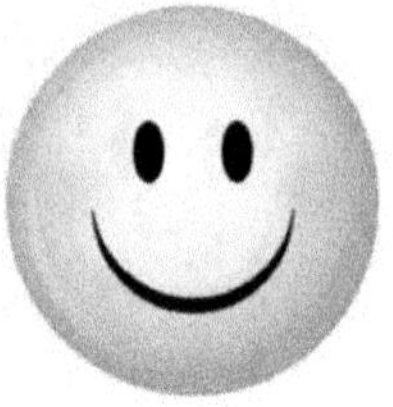

Join something outside of work.

Do something nice for someone
at work today.
Without expecting
anything in return.
Soon you will have
more friends at work
than you can count.

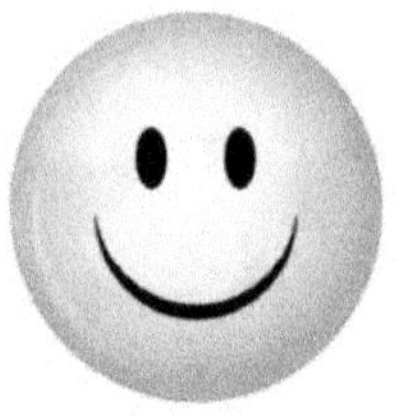

Have meetings around round tables. It diffuses hierarchy and encourages everyone to participate.

If someone or something at work
upsets you,
stop, breathe and count to 10
before you react.
Stay calm.

Breathe...

It's O.K. to ask for help.

Your writing should be simple.
Like Hemingway.

"Write the best story that you can and write it as straight as you can." - Ernest Hemingway

Your conversations should be
clear and simple.
Not everyone understands
big words.

What is *your* BIG IDEA for your company?
Share it!

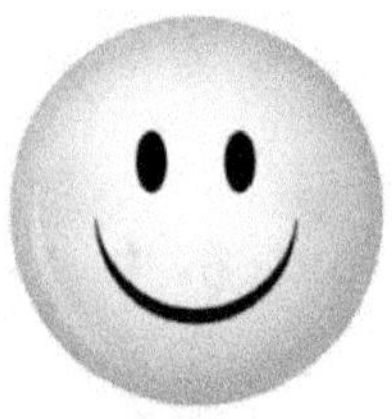

Walk in someone else's shoes.
You will expand your perspective.

The more you share information
with others,
the more trust you will build.

TRUST

Sometimes you will be smarter
than your Boss.
Accept it.
Don't dwell on it.

It's O.K. to say…
"I don't know."
Just follow it with…
"But I will find out and
get back to you."

It's O.K. to delegate.
You will not appear weak.
Rather, you will
become a better leader.

It's O.K. to say...

NO.

You know how much you can handle.

Be respectful and exhibit
professional behavior
to everyone in *all* situations.
Interpretation: Don't lose it!

Instead of conflict, try compromise.

Work on a project with a team.
It's can be more effective,
and more fun!

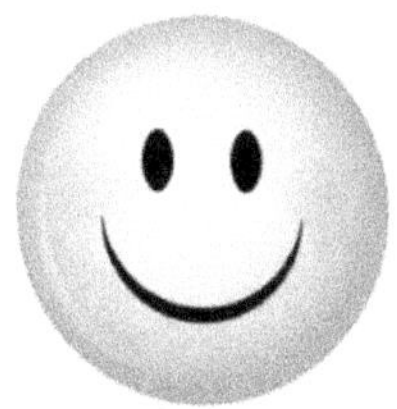

Inject some FUN into your workday.

- Suggest a ping pong table
- Pizza Fridays
- Scavenger hunt
- Create a *fun board* in the company kitchen where anyone can post ideas.

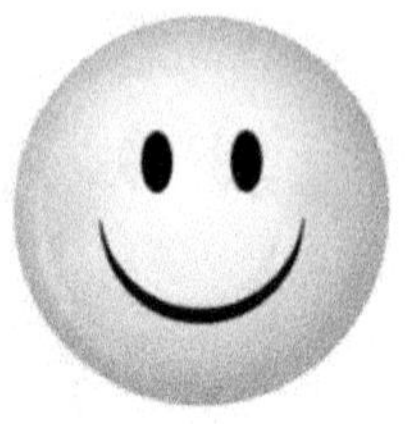

Reward yourself each day
for good work.
Even if the reward is small.
You will stay inspired.

Volunteer in the community.
With your team.
You will feel more connected.

If your job is not an ideal fit, talk with your manager and design your perfect position.

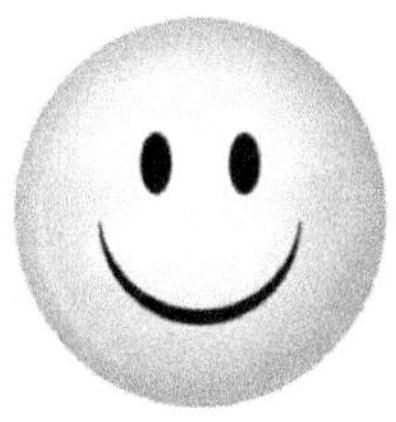

Do you feel happy when you
are valued?
Then value others and
watch happiness reflected back.

How do you balance
work, family, fun?

If you want to be happy at work,
you have to invest in
the rest of your life too.

Don't just sell your company's
products or services.
Solve customer problems and
you will be more successful.

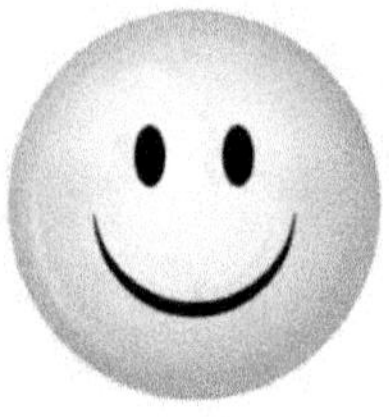

Keep notes on every meeting so you don't forget.

Talk to co-workers about *them*.
You'll gain friends
and mentors quickly.

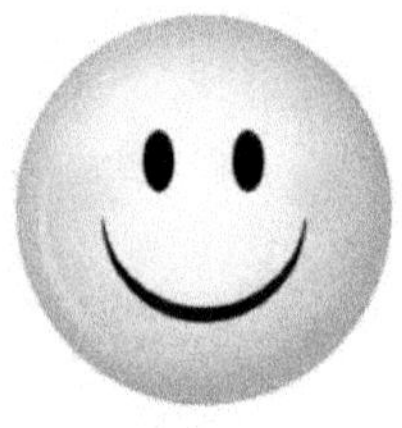

In a meeting…
Never hide your hands
under the table.
Never cross your arms.
Never turn your back.
Lean in…

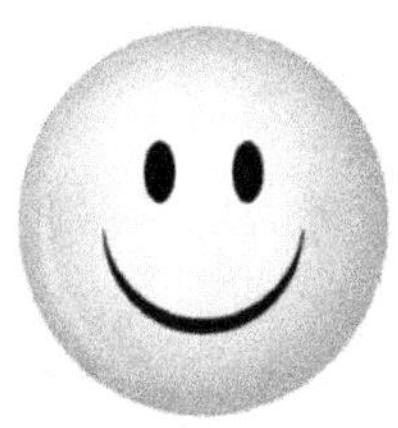

Ask questions.
Don't interrupt.
Maintain eye contact.
Don't fidget.
Be interested.

The more you learn
about your company,
The better decisions you will make.

If you feel lonely at work, reach out to a co-worker and ask them to meet for lunch or coffee. You'll make a new friend and be instantly happier.

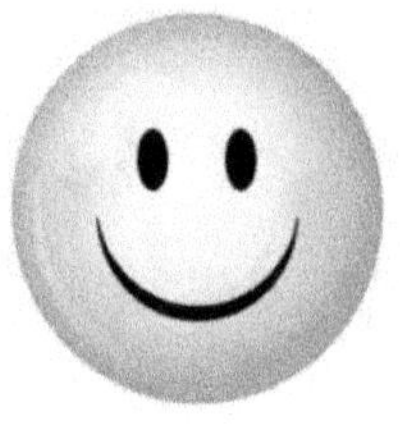

Don't ever be afraid to
share your ideas.

If you are a dedicated worker and
believe that you deserve a raise…
You probably do.
Have a collaborative conversation
with your Boss and ask for one.

Ask others for their input.
Two minds equal three times the output.

1+1=3

Make your workspace, cubicle
or office happy.
Share some of your personality.

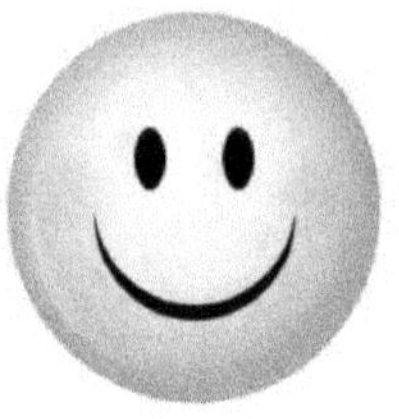

Part Three

Your Success

The best advice ever was from a 96-year-old Grandma who was the *only* woman she knew that worked.

Grandma, what is the secret to happiness at work?

"Do your own thing"

Some of the greatest leaders and happiest people in the world have reached their peak because of advice like Grandma gave.

Don't be afraid to carve your own path in life. You will be happier when you do.

Doing what you love is
the key to work happiness.
If you do, the money will follow.
Not the other way around.

"The only way to do great work is to love what you do. If you haven't found it, keep looking. Don't settle."

- Steve Jobs

Dream big and then break your dream into bite size pieces that you can accomplish each day.
Soon you will achieve, believe and be on to your next big dream.

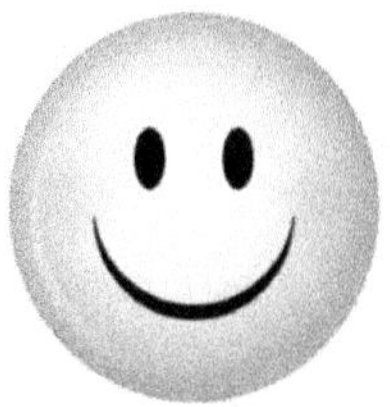

Always give more than
is asked of you.

Perceived obstacles along your career path are not obstacles. They are opportunities.

You have no control over yesterday.
It is done.

You have no control over tomorrow.
It will never come.

Your *only* power is in today.

Make it great and every tomorrow will become your best today.

If you want to get promoted,
start training your replacement.

The meaningful accomplishments in your life will matter much more than money.

Seek meaning.

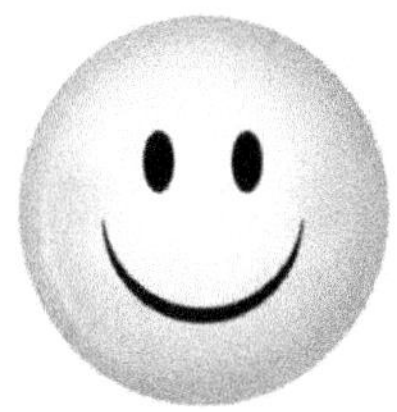

Don't always be the smartest one in
the room.
How will you grow?

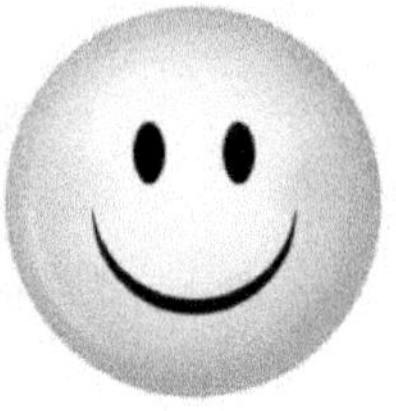

Praise is not as important as realizing your ideas.

If you only strive for is money,
you will always be chasing it.

Don't *ever* let failure stop you.

Stop climbing the ladder.
Hold the ladder instead.
You'll make lots of friends
along the way and
Sail to the top.

It's O.K. to have weaknesses.
Hidden inside is
your greatest strength.

EFFORT

=

SUCCESS

Choose one thing and
be the best you can
at that one thing.
Success will be yours.

1 BIG THING

Millionaires give more value to
others than themselves.
Always seek to help
solve other's problems.

PERSIST.

PERSIST.

PERSIST.

Even the most successful people
in the world
feel insecure sometimes.

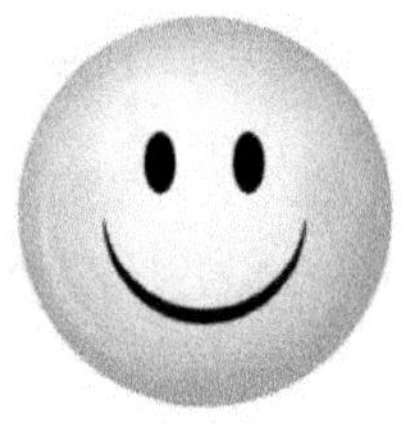

If you want to be successful….

Never stop…

Inventing
Creating
Learning
Helping

Life teaches you more than school.
Pay attention.

Keep moving forward.

Stay Curious.

Networking is a good way to market yourself without sounding like a sales pitch. Have conversations.

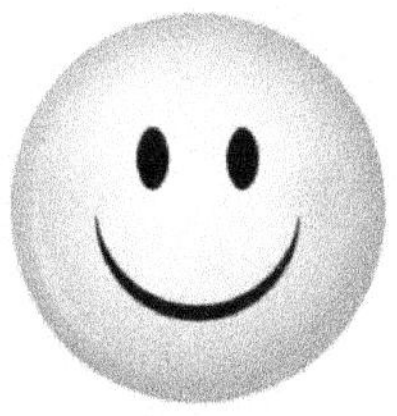

Negative people will
only bring you problems.
Stay clear.

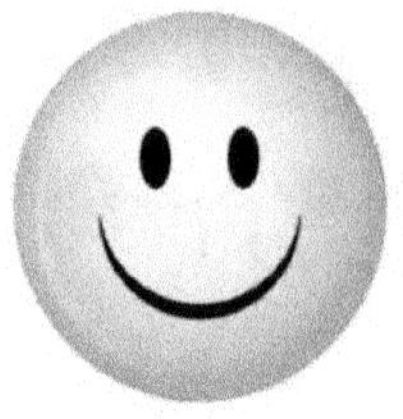

Don't post anything on social media
that you don't want
your employer to see.

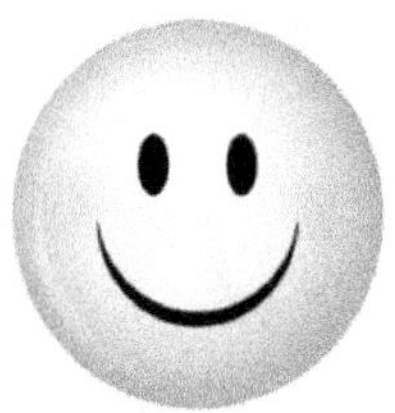

Your imagination is your greatest asset.

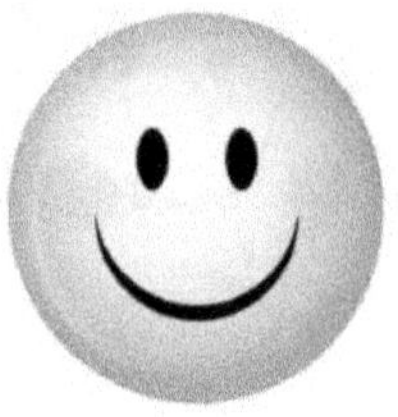

Forgive, and most of all…
FORGET.
Don't hang on to the negative past.

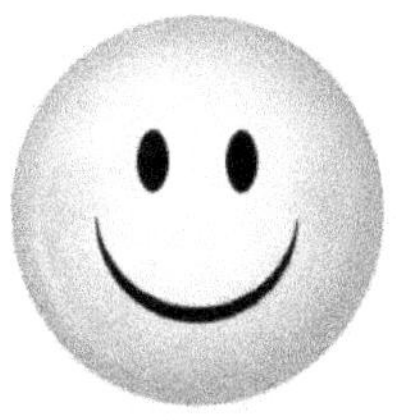

Always be *honest*.
Always be *authentic*.
Always be *kind*.

Everyone has the same
amount of time.
There are no exceptions.
If you use your time wisely,
you will rise highly.

Dreams are more powerful
than facts.

Life is a miracle.
Lives yours that way.

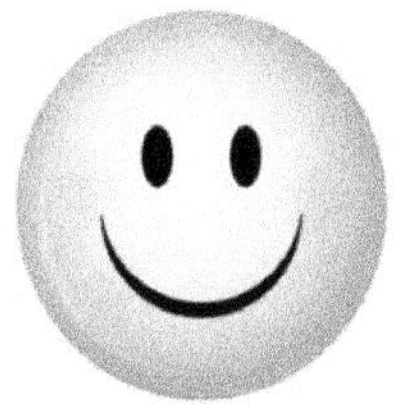

Practice gratitude instead of self-pity.

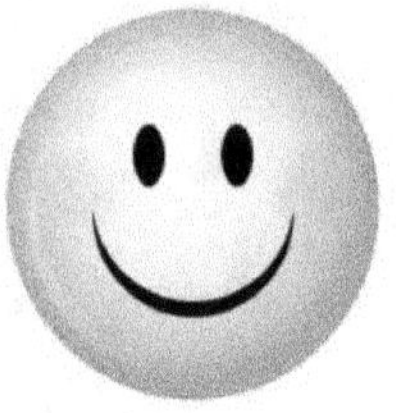

Mistakes are O.K. as long as you learn from them and don't repeat.

Know the 80-20 rule and then
break it as you go.
80% of your income will come
from 20% of your clients.

80/20

Sometimes the best advice is to *not* follow the crowd.

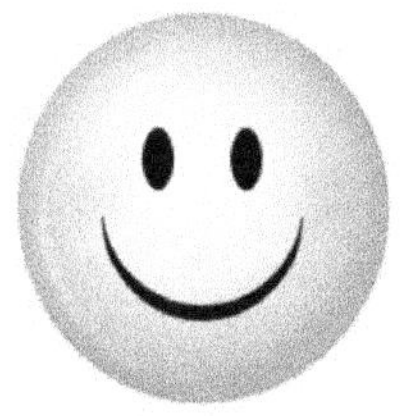

70, 80, 90 % of success
is simply showing up.

Show up.

Check your ego at the door.

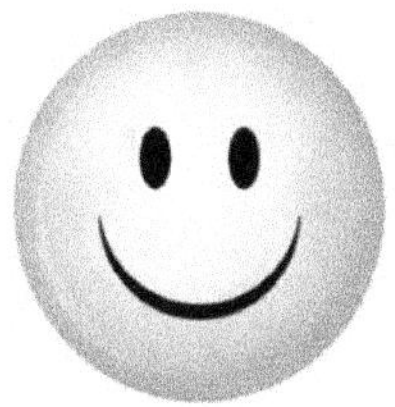

Some companies give awards
for top achievers.
Some give awards for top helpers.
Be a top helper and
you will achieve more.

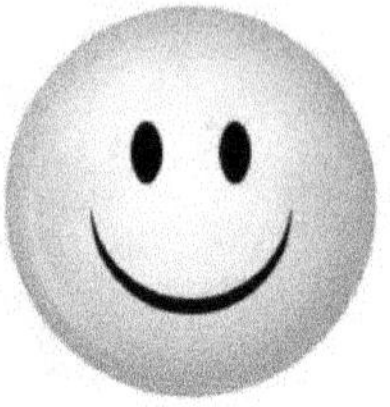

Always ask for the order.

Always say…

"Thank you!"

Always.

NEVER GIVE UP.
NEVER.
EVER.
NEVER GIVE UP.

The most successful people don't think the world owes them anything.

Be patient.
Success does not happen immediately.
Unless you win the lottery.
Then again…money is not the only measure of success.

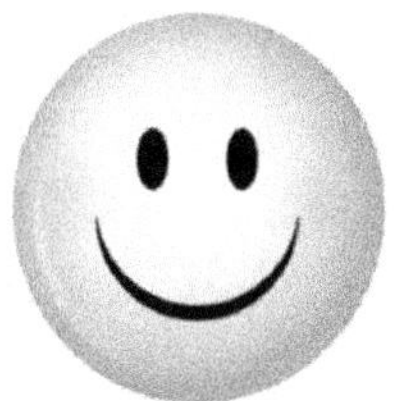

If you provide value, technology will never take away your job.

Seeing a client in person always
wins over emails, texts
or phone calls.

Be the kind of leader that people
want to work for.

Don't invade someone's
personal space.
3 feet away is a good rule to follow.

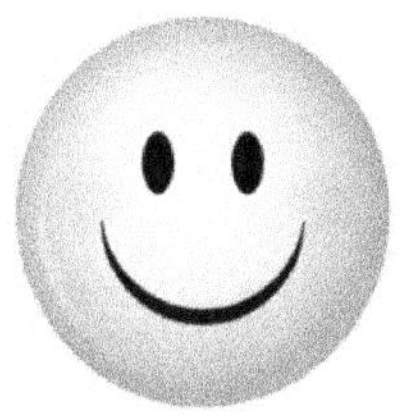

Engaged workers are happier.

ENGAGE!

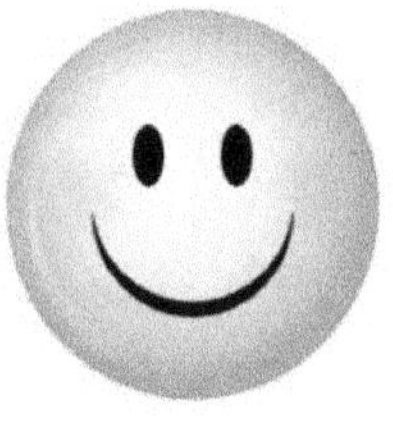

You know the golden rule.
Practice it.

Be nice to, and appreciate, everyone.
From the Janitor to the C.E.O.

Kindness & Opportunity
Will come back to you from the
most unexpected places.

Mistakes are O.K. as long as you learn from them and don't repeat.

Did you see this earlier?

Even if you repeat, it's O.K. Just don't repeat *again*.

Then it's no longer a mistake. It's sloppiness.

Keep your promises.

Do not fear rejection.
What's the worst thing
that can happen?

No two people have
the same fingerprints.
Be unique.

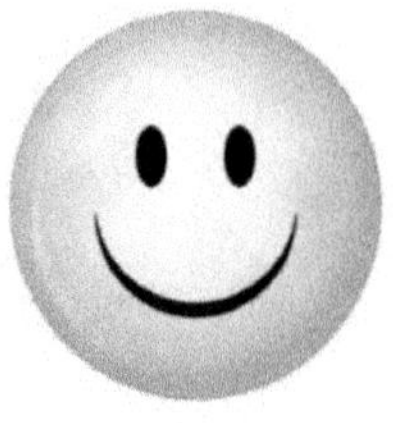

Emotional intelligence is more important than having a wall full of educational degrees. Use yours.

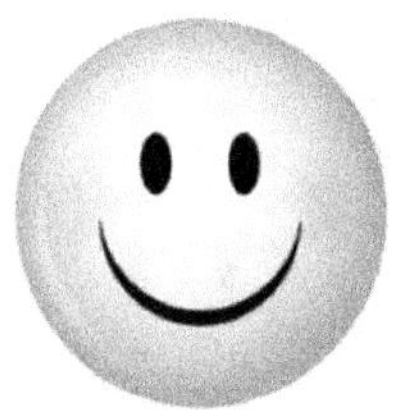

Don't be a Dictator of people.
Be a Curator.

Approach every conversation
as though it is
the most important one
you will ever have.

It's O.K. to use silence as a tool. Sometimes what you don't say is more powerful.

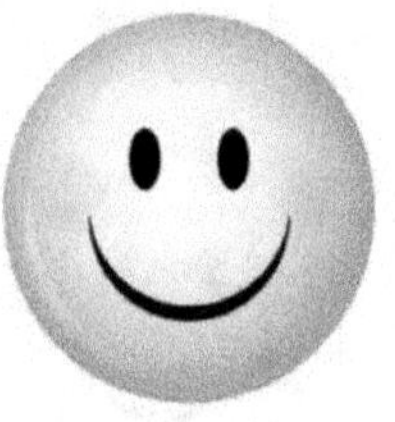

Don't cut corners.
Do the research.

Always be 5 minutes early.

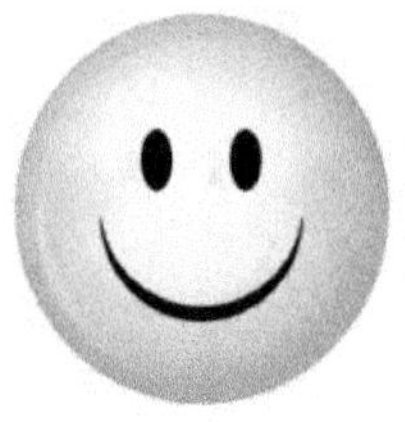

Do the thing you *least* want to do
first.
The rest of your day
will be a breeze.

If you can pinpoint the problem,
the answer will come much quicker.

Someone else shouting your praise is 10x more powerful.

Life is a marathon.
Not a 100-yard dash.
Be patient with yourself.
You are on your way.

There are always signs
along your path.
It's up to you to recognize them
and follow them
toward work happiness.

You may change jobs 5 or more
times in your life.
That *does not mean*
you are a failure.
You are evolving.

Don't make your happiness
conditional.
If I get this or that, *then* I'll be happy.
Strive to *feel* happy first,
and what you desire will follow.

Never criticize others.
Never.
Ever.
Never criticize others.

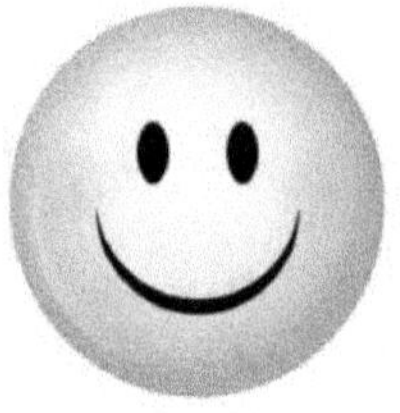

Only *you* know if you've
done your best.
So do your best.

You are great at something.
Keep looking until you find it!

Your future is BRIGHT!
Believe it!

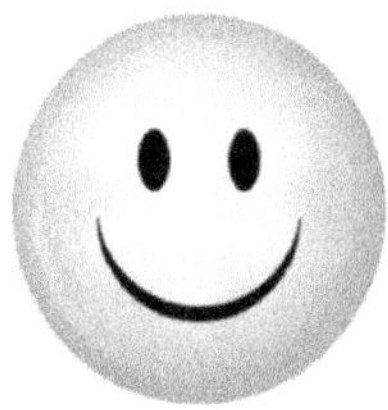

Life is a balancing act.
Take time to balance yours.

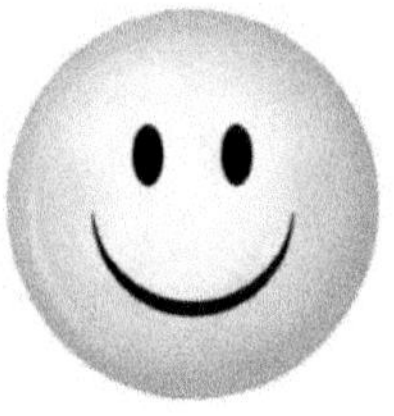

One of the best feelings in the world is when you can say…

Do 3 important things today.

It doesn't sound like much, but soon you'll achieve all your goals and will want to create new ones.

3

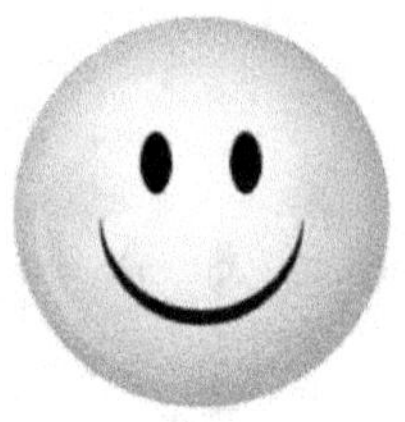

If you think you
are going to succeed,
you will…
If you think you are going to fail,
you will…
Choose success.

When you face a problem, think about how you can turn it into an opportunity.

Choose the kind of person you want to be in work and in life. Stick to that intention.

Ask WHY often.
You will make better decisions.

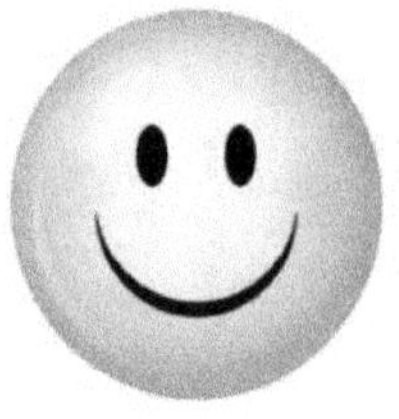

When you use the
IF-THEN strategy,
you can predict better outcomes.

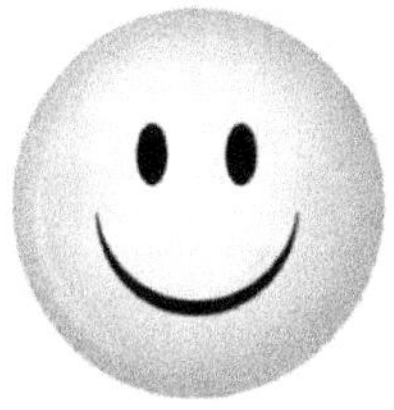

Seek out different experiences that
can be additive to
achieving your goals.
Don't just follow one road.

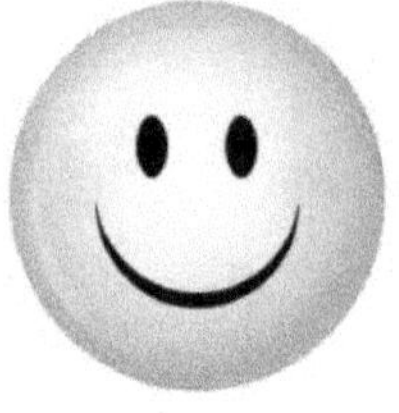

Do something new.
Sometimes scary.
Always exciting.

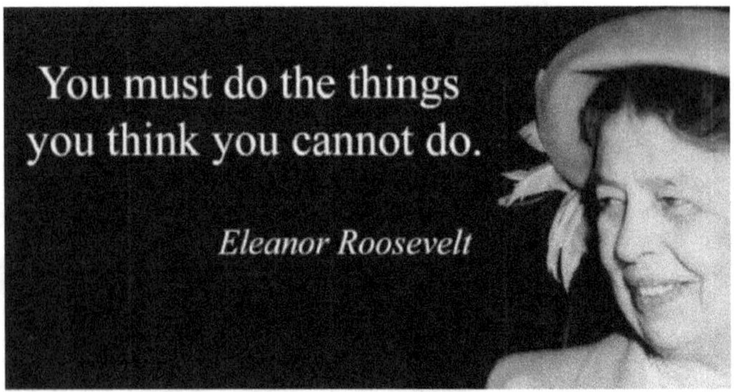

Vision boards
can help you see and feel
your success.
Make one.

Always do the right thing.

You are always moving forward.
You are always on the right path.

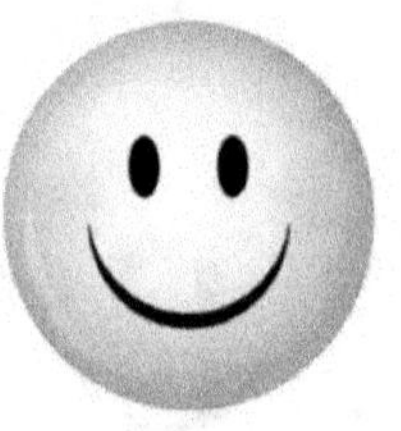

To be a great mentor you must…

 *Listen*

 *Ask*

 *Encourage*

 *Challenge*

Slow down.
Think.
Reflect.

Don't make life complicated.
Simplify.

Use both sides of your brain to create your best work.

Ask for testimonials and recommendations along the way. They will add up and be very valuable to you throughout your working life.

GREAT JOB!

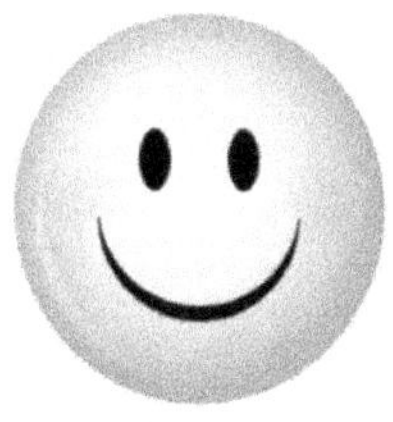

Set goals for the week,
month and year.

MY GOALS

1.
2.
3.

If you have the *will* to succeed….
You will.

You *CAN* change your world.

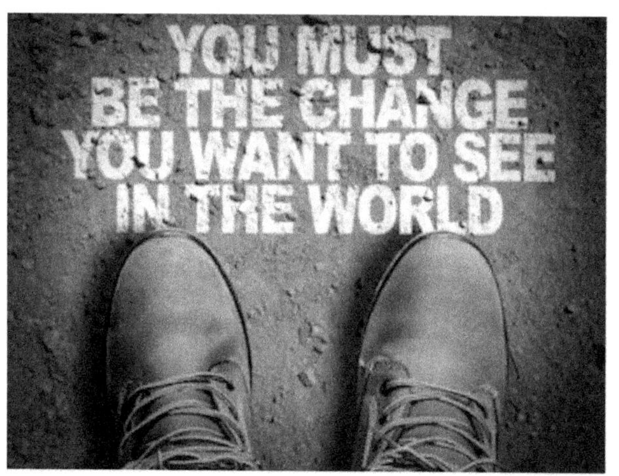

About the Author

Jody is the CEO of a Work Happiness Consultancy Firm.

She is a **TEDx** Speaker. Her idea worth sharing challenges everyone to step beyond the outer limits of their comfort zone to effect lasting, positive change.

At the time of this printing, Jody's **TEDx** talk has more than 500,000 views.

Jody is also an international Author and Speaker, writes for many publications including Entrepreneur, CEO Magazine and Thrive Global, and is interviewed on television, radio and podcasts regularly.

Learn more about her at:
www.jodybmiller.com

"If you've found this book helpful in guiding you toward a happier work life, please consider leaving a short review on Amazon."

*"You might also enjoy some of Jody's other books. **'From Drift to SHIFT – How Change Can Bring True Meaning and Happiness to your work and life,'** and a Novel she wrote under JB Miller, **'No Time For Love.'***

The MISOGI Method: The Way To Achieve Lasting Happiness and Success (based on Jody's TEDx talk) will be out soon! Email her if you would like to be on the launch list.

jody@jodybmiller.com

READ ON FOR A SAMPLE OF BOOK TWO IN THE BIG LITTLE BOOK OF SERIES.

BIG little books Being Released in 2019

the BIG little book of…
relationship happiness
the BIG little book of…
meditation happiness
the BIG little book of…
fitness happiness
the BIG little book of…
health happiness
the BIG little book of…
friendship happiness
the BIG little book of…
personal happiness

the BIG
little book
of
relationship
happiness
jody b. miller
TEDx Speaker, Author of the BIG little book of...series
"The MISOGI Method: The Way To Achieve Lasting Happiness"

the BIG little book of relationship happiness

jody b. miller

TEDx Speaker, Author of
"the BIG little book of..." series
"The MISOGI Method: The Way To Achieve Lasting Happiness"

the BIG little book of relationship happiness

Published By
Alskar Publishing
P.O. Box 2637, Santa Barbara, CA 93120

Website: www.jodybmiller.com
Email: jody@jodybmiller.com

Layout by: JC Berry
Photos: Licensed

First published: January, 2019

ISBN-13: 978-1-7335352-3-6
E-Book

Dedication

I am so glad we found each other again after all these years.

Sample Chapter of Book Two

the BIG little book of relationship happiness

written by Jody B. Miller

Alskar Publishing
U.S.A.

From the Author

The advice in this BIG little book comes from decades of life experience, research, listening to thousands of happy and unhappy people in relationships, and from curating the best advice from Ph.D.'s, Psychologists and Psychiatrists from around the world.

It's all about helping you lead a life of relationship happiness.

For best results, pick and choose the advice that best fits your situation and apply to your life immediately.

Repeat as needed.

Part One

Self-Love

Part Two

Romance

Part Three

Friendship

If you find true love, even once in
your life,
you have found happiness.

For your relationship to last, you must not only love your partner, you must *like* them too.

Going to bed angry is
not the worst thing.
It is better than
losing your composure.
Talk about it in the morning.

Talk about money *before*
you tie the knot.
Money issues can
make or break your relationship.

$$$$

Talk about having kids
before you tie the knot.
If you are not on
the same page about family,
you are not on the same page
about your relationship.

Keep a little of yourself *to* yourself.

If you want someone to love you
unconditionally,
you have to love yourself
unconditionally first.

Don't have sex on the first date.
You'll ruin everything!

Dating services are not all bad.
Don't stalk though…

When first starting out…
Go Dutch.

Don't go heavy right out of the gate.
Keep conversation light and fun.

Always keep 'girl' and 'guy' talk confidential.
Sometimes we just vent to figure things out.

Don't talk about your X until the relationship gets more serious. If you are asked, keep it general.

We grew apart.

or

We weren't on the same page.

If you have butterflies in your stomach,
that's a good sign!

If you have even one best friend in life, you have a life well-lived.

An Irish Blessing...

"MAY THE ROAD RISE TO MEET YOU,

AND THE WIND ALWAYS

BE AT YOUR BACK.

MAY THE SUN SHINE WARM

ON YOUR FACE

AND THE RAINS FALL SOFTLY ON YOUR FIELDS.

AND UNTIL WE MEET AGAIN...

MAY GOD HOLD YOU GENTLY IN THE PALM OF HIS HAND.

To get on the launch list for

---

the BIG little book of relationship happiness,

Email: jody@jodybmiller.com

In the subject line put: relationships to get a coupon.

www.ingramcontent.com/pod-product-compliance
Lightning Source LLC
LaVergne TN
LVHW051626080426
835511LV00016B/2189

* 9 7 8 1 7 3 3 5 3 5 2 2 9 *